Lead Your Team!

21 Leadership Lessons for Direct Selling

Randy Gage

Lead Your Team!
21 Leadership Lessons for Direct Selling

Copyright© MMXVI Randy Gage and Prime Concepts Group Inc.

All rights reserved. No part of this book may be reproduced or transmitted in any form by any means, electronic or mechanical, or by any information storage or retrieval system, without written permission from the publisher.

Visit networkmarketingtimes.com or randygage.com for more resources created by Randy Gage.

Table of Contents

Forward: Leaders Lead!............7

Lesson 1: Don't Set Yourself Up to Lose............13

Lesson 2: You Don't Buy Diamonds at a Flea Market 17

Lesson 3: Duplication Is Real............21

Lesson 4: Salesy Is Better Than Brokey 27

Lesson 5: Go All In or Quit Now............31

Lesson 6: Be the One to Choose............35

Lesson 7: Your Sponsor Doesn't Cash Your Checks 39

Lesson 8: The Lie of Objections............43

Lesson 9: It's Never About the Hype............47

Lesson 10: Stop Looking for Outside Validation............51

Lesson 11: Your Best Investment............57

Lesson 12: Present an Empowering Story............63

Lesson 13: Build to Critical Mass............69

Lesson 14: Become Amazing at Meeting People............73

Lesson 15: Become Beyond Amazing at Inviting............77

Lesson 16: Use the Two-Process System............85

Lesson 17: Solve Problems............89

Lesson 18: Kill Distractions!............93

Lesson 19: Own the Stage............97

Lesson 20: The Challenges on Your Path...Are the Path............101

Lesson 21: Fire Yourself!............105

Final Thoughts............110

Recommended Resources............111

FORWARD
LEADERS LEAD!

LEAD YOUR TEAM!

Forward
Leaders Lead!

A nonprofit organization I'm a member of launched an initiative to rename and rebrand the organization. Of course most people don't like change, so immediately the leadership faced some resistance in the form of badgering phone calls, outraged emails, and indignant updates on social media.

Within a week or two, the leaders of the organization cancelled all changes, formed committees to do nothing, and kept everything comfortably the way it was. They crumpled like a cheap suit.

I guess they thought making bold changes would receive instant, unanimous, and reassuring acclaim from everyone.

But that's not how it works in the real world…

Leadership isn't putting out popular proposals to universal praise. It requires being a critical thinker, creating a vision for the future, sometimes – oftentimes – before the people they lead even see it for themselves. In other words…

Leaders lead.

One of my consulting clients recently took over a 40-year-old organization that hasn't been relevant in a long time. He prides himself on being a consensus builder. Which means he's frantically working to build consensus.

So the advice I gave him shocked him…

I told him the organization he inherited didn't need a consensus builder. They need someone to burn down the fucking barn.

Don't get me wrong. Consensus is good. Most of the time. But there are other times when consensus is simply a code word for mediocrity. Consensus usually comes about to keep everyone comfortable. However, if you want to do something astonishing, you need to be willing to get uncomfortable.

Mediocrity can be managed. Excellence must be led.

And real leaders often ruffle feathers, rattle molars, and just generally make people uncomfortable. Because if they didn't need you to do those things – they wouldn't need a leader in the first place.

Real leadership is scary. For the leader and those being led. It's scary because there is something at stake: Greatness.

People look to leaders because they want someone who challenges them to have a higher vision and strive to accomplish more, whether for themselves or a noble purpose. If the thing you endeavor to do doesn't hurt a little, involve risk, or scare you – it's probably not a goal worthy of you.

Real leadership has nothing to do with finding your "leadership style." That's the feel-good pabulum you read in leadership books written by people who have never actually led anything.

The question is not what leadership style suits your personality – but what leadership style the people you are leading need.

Sometimes that's being a consensus builder. Sometimes it means reengaging past leaders, making everyone feel safe, and keeping people focused. But more often, leadership means being the one to give the wake-up call, letting people know the current situation is no longer acceptable, and challenging them to become more. And when an organization is in those straights, it doesn't need consensus builders. It needs leaders to lead.

Now let's explore all this in the context of network marketing and dissect what leadership looks like in our space…

Guess what? The direct selling and network marketing business is changing. A lot. And it's about to change much more in dramatic and powerful ways. So why can you walk into almost any hotel opportunity meeting room on a Tuesday evening and see the same presentation you would have seen in the 90s? Or even the 80s?

We're in the decade of the most cataclysmic changes in human history. Yet most people in our profession haven't recognized that they need to change as well.

I've been in this game for more than thirty years; operating at a pretty high level for the last fifteen or twenty. I've been a top producer, consulted on the corporate level, and personally coached the top income earners in dozens of different companies. So this has provided a fascinating perspective on the business and how it is evolving. The demographics of who is participating have changed greatly, and so has the profile of the type of people who become successful.

Social media and the Internet have upended a lot of old-school practices. Mobile apps are blowing up the process even more. Government regulatory standards have evolved. Our societal norms and culture have as well.

So it's a bold new world we operate in. Which is the reason I wrote this book...

To help people like you – those who want to lead a large team and provide the kind of inspiring and empowering leadership our profession so desperately needs right now.

You don't need a stronger upline. *You need to become your own upline.* Because true leadership begins with leading yourself.

We're running an all-volunteer army here. No one gets drafted. They have to choose to enlist. Which means you have to model the behavior and become the kind of leader that people will want to follow.

Leadership is the ability to cause people to willingly do things they wouldn't ordinarily want to do.

Think about it. Who joins our business and wants to speak in front of a large group of people? Almost no one. In fact, most have an acute fear of public speaking. But what happens?

They see leaders making hotel presentations or conducting training and want to become like them. Their desire to become a leader becomes stronger than their fear of speaking.

How many people buy their first suit or tie because they are inspired by the example of someone in the sponsorship line? Think of the people who develop – and actually love – self-discipline in our profession.

And that is the true essence of what you must do as a leader. Model behavior that others will want to emulate. Fuel the desire they have to live their dreams and become stronger than their fear of doing this.

This book is actually the result of a radio interview I did a while back. The host asked me – if I could go back in time, what would I say to my younger self?

If I could go back 30 years and speak to that nervous young man with social anxiety disorder that joined the business, desperate to get rich – these are the lessons I would want to share with him.

This advice would help him understand he could be good enough to succeed, and he would end up helping many others along the way. I would try to convey that the business is much more than the money, trips, and exotic cars. I would want him (and you) to know, that this is a journey that can transform one's life.

I wouldn't want to eliminate challenges for my younger self. Those were the stepping stones that caused me to learn skills, develop character, and build courage. But I would want him, and you, to know in the darkest hours, there will be breakthroughs along the way. And the journey is well worth it.

So here's what I want to tell you…

Randy Gage
March, 2017 Miami Beach, Florida

LESSON 1
DON'T SET YOURSELF UP TO LOSE

LEAD YOUR TEAM!

Lesson 1
Don't Set Yourself Up to Lose

Picture this scenario: Someone is in a dead-end career or job. They know they will have to work 45 or 50 years without any real satisfaction, struggle to get by, and then retire on half of what they used to make.

They get an opportunity in our profession to take their life back and create financial freedom for themselves. For the first time in their life, they have the opportunity to create real options for the future.

It won't happen overnight. To build something real in our business takes solid work and actual time. People who produce extraordinary results can create a solid business with residual income in two years. For most serious people, it will take four or five years.

Now four or five years is no joke. That takes dedication, determination and resilience. But the payoff is worth it. Undisputedly worth it.

We are talking about investing four or five years in creating a residual income stream that can provide freedom and security for the rest of your life.

But what happens far too often?

Someone joins our business and goes through a few months of learning. They are not a millionaire by month two, so they drop out. To do what? To go back to working 45 or 50 years without any real satisfaction, struggle to get by, and then retire on half of what they used to make.

This is totally crazy behavior. But it happens in our business all the time. And that means we haven't done our job as leaders, creating the right expectations.

One thing you should know is that your business will never be more difficult than it is at the beginning. The first month is the hardest. The first *week* is the hardest. But often the difficulty of these earliest struggles is disguised by the initial excitement and hope we bring into the business. As that euphoria wears off, people often assign too much emphasis to the struggles and lose sight of the long game.

Make sure you know that the beginning of your business will be the hardest. Teach your people the same thing. And when you face the challenges, which you most definitely will, keep them in perspective.

Okay, your hot prospect never showed up for the presentation. That's cute.

Okay, someone you signed up last week decided to quit. Is the world coming to an end?

Okay, a prospect refused to watch your video. Is that the worst thing that happened to you today? Seriously?

Somewhere in your town today, a person just got a devastating medical diagnosis. Someone lost a loved one in a tragic accident. Others are facing foreclosures and bankruptcy.

You've had challenges. I get that. You'll have more. You

need to get that. Learn from those challenges. Use them as stepping stones to become the person and leader you are meant to be.

No one dies when you get rejected; nothing tragic is going to happen.

The important thing to remember: The business will only get easier the longer you stay in it.

The people who drop out in the early stages throw away the investment they made in their future to go back to one they already had rejected as inadequate.

So please don't set yourself up to lose. If you're not willing to give the business a fair chance and the real time required – meaning four or five years to create something substantial – please don't waste your time. And if you have already started, don't give up!

LESSON 2
YOU DON'T BUY DIAMONDS AT THE FLEA MARKET

LEAD YOUR TEAM!

Lesson 2
You Don't Buy Diamonds at a Flea Market

Let's suppose you're a dashing young man, and you've found the girl of your dreams. You want to marry her and live happy ever after. If you want to discover the perfect diamond engagement ring, you go to a fine jeweler. You don't buy diamonds at a flea market. Cause if you do, they're probably not going to be real.

If you want to climb a mountain, would you find someone who stopped halfway and ask them how to reach the summit?

If you wanted to learn to fly, would you seek advice from someone who crashed and had their pilot's license revoked?

If you wanted to become a doctor, would you ask someone who played the part on TV?

Of course not.

But are you asking advice on network marketing from your brother-in-law who was in Herbalife for six weeks back in the 90s?

Do you realize how many of your new team members do exactly that?

The most dangerous position to be in is usually when you don't know what you don't know, because your ignorance prevents you from seeking out the correct guidance you really need. That's the situation when people are new in the business.

They are starting a new profession and have no experience in it. They ask around, looking for advice from anyone willing to offer it. This can be a great mistake.

Because who is usually the first person to offer "expert" advice?

The person who failed at the business in the past. Certainly there is a group of people who tried the business, faced some challenges, and dropped out without giving it a chance. They simply weren't prepared or willing to do what is required to succeed.

Now if you ask advice from these people, how many do you think will believe that their failure was their own fault? And how many do you believe their lack of success was entirely attributed to outside factors, like the business doesn't work?

There's an even bigger group of town criers out there. These are the people who never learned the difference between an illegal pyramid or money game and a legitimate network marketing or direct selling company. They joined something that was NOT network marketing and guaranteed to fail. But they have no idea that what they attempted wasn't even actually a network marketing business. And unfortunately this doesn't stop them from telling everyone in their world that the model simply doesn't work.

So let's think about this clearly. If you are new in the business, the only people who can give you any meaningful advice are the people who have already been successful in the business.

People who have accomplished the very thing you desire to achieve.

There are many people who want to speak into your life. The key is having the discernment to know who to allow in.

LESSON 3
DUPLICATION IS REAL

LEAD YOUR TEAM!

Lesson 3
Duplication Is Real

The phone rang and it was Ivan, a good friend who happened to be cross-line with the same sponsor as I. He was looking for some friendly advice about a major event he had coming up. He had secured a very large convention hall and hadn't sold many tickets. He stood to be on the hook for a large amount of money and was frantically looking for what he could do to mitigate the damage.

I started talking about some ways in which he might create serious and sustainable duplication in the next couple weeks to charge up his ticket sales. Then he asked me a fascinating question:

"But is duplication really real?"

My first reaction was shock. I was genuinely astonished he asked this question. And immediately inquired what caused him to wonder about something I take as for granted as gravity.

He then shared that our mutual sponsor had told him duplication didn't really exist. That it was a delusion only I had. Which shouldn't have surprised me...

Our sponsor never really had much time for the fundamentals and mechanics of the business. He preferred to recruit by going "whale hunting," looking for distributors from other companies with large groups he could entice to switch over to his team.

He's certainly not alone in that. Many people (and companies) build their entire strategy around poaching people with large teams from other companies. Doing so can make a big impact short-term, but I've never been impressed with the long-term results.

First off is the issue of the overall health of the profession. Instead of fighting with other company distributors over a piece of the pie, wouldn't it make more sense to work together building a bigger pie? There are more than six billion people in the world who aren't even in network marketing. Why don't we offer them the opportunity?

In isolated cases, there will be leaders in a company that have realized it is necessary to move on. After ten years working with a program I loved, the company was sold. I couldn't sign off on the direction the new ownership group was taking the company and felt morally obligated to resign.

I have a friend who built a large team in another company. The founder turned it over to his daughter and she made some decisions that ultimately led to the company no longer paying commissions.

These types of situations happen all the time. And if you are fortunate enough to have a relationship with someone at the moment they decide they need to find a new home, that change can work out great for the pair of you.

But let's be honest: That's a one-of situation other people can't duplicate. So celebrate these circumstances when they occur, but don't try to build a business plan on them.

If you want to build a large team, you have to do the blocking and tackling – the real day-to-day work of constructing a strong team with a vibrant customer base.

And you want to do it in a way that the people you bring into the business can replicate. That is duplication. And yes, duplication is real.

Duplication means building in a duplicable way, using a system that allows everyone to replicate the same results. In terms of practical application, this means you have standard operating processes in place for each phase of the business: recruiting, training, customer acquisition, and leadership development.

So, for example, you want to have a standard process on how you obtain customers. A step-by-step process on how you present the business opportunity to candidates. A standardized presentation, a template for training new distributors and a model for how people advance into team leadership.

A few years back, I was lying deathly ill in a room in Moscow, guarded around the clock by two bodyguards. They suspected that I had been poisoned by the mafia there. (Which while a fascinating story, will have to wait for another book!) The point being, I was in bed, taking no phone calls or emails for the final four days of the month. And that month I broke the highest rank anyone in the company had ever achieved.

Fast-forward a few years later. I took a two-year sabbatical.

One week after I came back, I broke a higher rank. Again a rank no one else in the world had ever achieved up until that point.

How did that happen?

Duplication. By having a system, tools and processes that everyone on the team could follow. Creating a track that allowed my people to step into their own greatness and leadership abilities. Remember, it's never about you and what you can do. The magic happens when you figure out what you can do, that facilitates how your people can achieve their dreams in the business.

That's duplication. It's real. And it is vital that you create it –not only for yourself, but for your team.

I can give you a trio of resources to help you ensure that you and your team are building in a way that produces optimal duplication. Let's look at them:

1. How to Build a Multi-Level Money Machine
This is considered by many leaders to be the seminal work on building a solid, strong team. In its fourth edition, this book is still current with the market today. Make it part of your training system with your team.

2. The Duplication Nation Audio or Video Album
This will show you exactly how to build a step-by-step system for your team to follow. There are twelve modules on every aspect of building the business.

3. Academy for Network Marketing Leadership
This is an online learning platform that gives you access to training

24/7. You can watch the course for any specific action you need to take right then. And it includes "Randy's Rocket Boosters" for when you need an extra dose of inspiration or courage. This resource is designed to promote leadership – yours and the potential leaders on your team. I have a special offer for readers of this book, where you can test drive the program the first month for only $1 instead of the normal registration fee.

I hope you'll utilize all three resources so you get the best results with the least effort and in the minimal amount of time. There are far too many people in the business already who don't really understand the concept of duplication. These are the "MLM grinders" who try to do everything themselves. They are the only ones that make presentations and lead the training for their team. The minute they stop working, everything unravels for them and their team.

You don't want that to happen for you...

There are a couple things you need to be cognizant of. First, one of your sacred responsibilities as a leader is to never do anything for a team member that they are capable of doing themselves. And second, your primary job is to work yourself out of a job.

So recognize that duplication is real and it's possible. But it won't happen by itself. You must be mindful of the way you build the business, so you create a pattern of actions that others can replicate. That is the greatest gift you can provide as a leader for your team.

LESSON 4
SALESY IS BETTER THAN BROKEY

LEAD YOUR TEAM!

Lesson 4
Salesy Is Better Than Brokey

Remember in the Foreword we discussed how the business has changed over the decades? Well, that's probably true in no area more than the selling aspect.

In the 80s and 90s, people said that selling didn't matter. (I know, because I was one of them.) We talked about how volume was created by the personal consumption of the network. And there was truth in that.

Huge volumes were produced by large teams. People may have been attracted by the allure of making money. But they became consumers as part of the process, and as a result, many lives were enhanced.

People lost weight, improved their complexion, gained more energy, saved money on family expenses, and probably lived longer lives.

Distributors in a company are much more compliant with following protocols and thus get better results. There are at least two generations of people on earth that were exposed to health and wellness through network marketing that probably would never have been without the business.

That's the good side. Unfortunately, there was the other side...

Companies that hyped the business opportunity and had no interest in what the product line was or did. Unscrupulous people who practice "front loading" by encouraging people to purchase huge initial inventories they never had a realistic chance of selling.

The other issue came when people (again, myself included) used to suggest that getting customers was a waste of time and people should focus all their efforts on recruiting only. This advice may have been well meaning, but it created a bad result: A culture that demeaned and diminished the value of the product line.

Finally came the issue of bringing in people who didn't want to sell. We were so desperate to enroll new business builders that we pandered to these people. We told them the business could be built without retailing or selling. And that's just not the case, particularly now.

Yes, You Have to (Get to) Sell

We can make analogies about how you recommend a great movie or restaurant, and we can talk about "sharing" all we want. The bottom line is, everyone needs to be willing and able to sell the product line. And needs to have a viable customer base of people who are not involved in the compensation plan.

In the 90s we might have been able to make the case that having customers outside the pay plan was a luxury. "Might" have been able to make that argument. But that certainly is not true today.

The regulatory environment has changed with cataclysmic ferocity. And the path is crystal clear. In places like the

United States of America, there are no governing national laws that regulate the profession. It's a patchwork of precedents, set by legal actions and consent decrees with various government agencies. And the most recent consent decrees signed by firms including Vemma and Herbalife most definitely create precedents for having a substantial percentage of people who are customers but don't receive any rewards from the compensation plan.

So it's time for a reset.

When someone tells you, "I want to make money, but I hate to sell and I would never market the products," accept that they are not a candidate for the business. Don't pander to them and don't tell them what they want to hear. (Which is that they can get rich without selling any products.)

People need to sell to be successful in our business. Actually they "get" to sell. So if they are not excited enough about the product or service to recommend it to the people in their world, they're not right for the business. And if YOU are not so excited about your product or service line that you want to promote it, find a new company or get out of the business. Otherwise you're wasting everyone's time.

LESSON 5
GO ALL IN OR QUIT NOW

LEAD YOUR TEAM!

Lesson 5
Go All In or Quit Now

Sometimes you have a prospect tell you something to the effect that they will try the business. And by "try" they mean they won't sign up or order product yet, but they'll present the idea to a few friends first. And if those friends think it's a good idea, they will enroll.

That dog don't hunt.

If someone tells me anything like that, I tell them the business isn't for them, thank them for their time, and move along. You need to do the same.

When someone hosts their first home meeting, makes their first presentation, or invites their initial prospects to any kind of presentation, they need to be enrolled, invested, and committed. Only then will they have any credibility and success with the people they invite to look at the business. And this is true for you as well...

Don't tiptoe into the business seeking approval from others as to whether you made a good decision.

Do your homework about the profession, the product line, your company and the sponsorship line. Make a decision based on what you discover.

If you're not sure the business is right for you, keep asking questions until you know for sure.

If you can't get there, don't join.

And if your decision is to move forward, then batten the hatches and set sail. Yes, ships are safe in the harbor. But that's not what ships are for.

LESSON 6
BE THE ONE TO CHOOSE

LEAD YOUR TEAM!

Lesson 6
Be the One to Choose

This is a follow-up to the last lesson about doing your homework. But I want to dig deeper because it reflects an interesting dynamic of the business.

For most people, their first time around, their company chooses them. That's because most people don't even know the business exists at that point. So their only perspective of the business is what's presented by this first potential sponsor and opportunity. If they don't get it, they don't join. If they're excited, they jump right in. They don't do any research about other companies or sponsors because that's not even in their thinking at that stage. They simply jump in.

Sometimes that works out great. And sometimes, not so much...

If you were chosen by a company and things didn't work out, there's no shame in that. The shame would be if you didn't learn from that.

Now you know better. You understand that this is a huge profession with hundreds of companies involved. Each has its own unique situation.

Every product line offers different opportunities and challenges. Every compensation plan rewards you differently for practicing the same behaviors. Each corporate team has different strengths and weaknesses. And every person offering to sponsor you into the business will help and hinder you in different ways.

Some sponsors will want you to join their team, then actually feel threatened by you and your accomplishments. Believe it or not, they may subconsciously (or even consciously) try to sabotage your efforts. Of course, this is foolish and counter-productive. But people do foolish and counter productive things every day.

Some sponsors will project their issues on you, dent your self-esteem, and hold you back. Others will recognize greatness in you that you don't even yet know is there. They will inspire you, challenge you and help you grow as an entrepreneur and as a person.

And others will simply be a nonfactor, neither obstructing your progress nor helping you move forward.

Some models that identify themselves as network marketing companies are actually money games, pyramid schemes or other hustles. Some companies focus all their energy on recruiting and the product line doesn't really matter to them. Some companies are totally devoted to providing an amazing product line, but they neglect the infrastructure required for you to do the business.

You have to be responsible for your own business. (More about that in the next lesson.) But the fact is, the company and sponsorship line you work with will have a direct impact on your ability to be successful. Some will make your job easier, others will make it more difficult.

That doesn't mean you should get distracted and start shopping around. If you're in a solid company, stay focused. But if circumstances change and you feel it is necessary to change companies, be mindful about choosing the company and team you want to work with.

Read the chapter in my *How to Build a Multi-Level Money Machine* book about selecting the right company. Choose your company the way you would if you were investing a million dollars to buy a franchise from them. And select your sponsor with the criteria of whether you want to spend the rest of your life working with them, traveling the world, and enjoying holidays together. Because if you choose right, that's exactly what will happen.

LESSON 7
YOUR SPONSOR DOESN'T CASH YOUR CHECKS

LEAD YOUR TEAM!

Lesson 7

Your Sponsor Doesn't Cash Your Checks

A fascinating insight emerged when I was sitting around a table with about ten other million-dollar-plus producers. One by one, people started regaling the group with their war stories of the horrible sponsors they had had. One thing became apparent as the pattern developed…

Each of us felt that having a weak sponsor had made us stronger.

Being a sponsor is a lot like being a parent. If you're a "helicopter parent," always hovering around your children protecting them, they miss out on some important life lessons. It's no different in our business.

One of the philosophies I operate with is to never do anything for a team member that they are capable of doing themselves. You don't want to solve problems for your people. You want to teach them how to solve problems for themselves.

Now think about the dynamic when you're on the other end…

It seems you want your sponsor to do things for you, solve your problems and make things easier. But that's not always your highest good. There are some lessons you will need to learn yourself. And actions you must take yourself.

If you think the secret to success is getting spillover from your sponsorship line, you're going to be momentously disappointed. Because no matter what kind of compensation plan you are working with, it will always still have personal enrollment and volume requirements. As it should.

The role of your sponsorship line is to guide you, teach you and hopefully, nurture and develop your inherent talents. Their job is to show you the path to success, but they can't travel it for you.

A lot of people have an entitlement mentality. They believe because their sponsorship line receives overrides on their volume, that sponsorship line is responsible for building their business. But that is not the case.

You are the one who gets the majority of the income from your distributorship. The bonus checks are going to be in your name, not your sponsor's.

Your distributorship can become a valuable asset, a profit-generating business you can bequeath to your children or grandchildren. So take personal responsibility to build, maintain, and grow it.

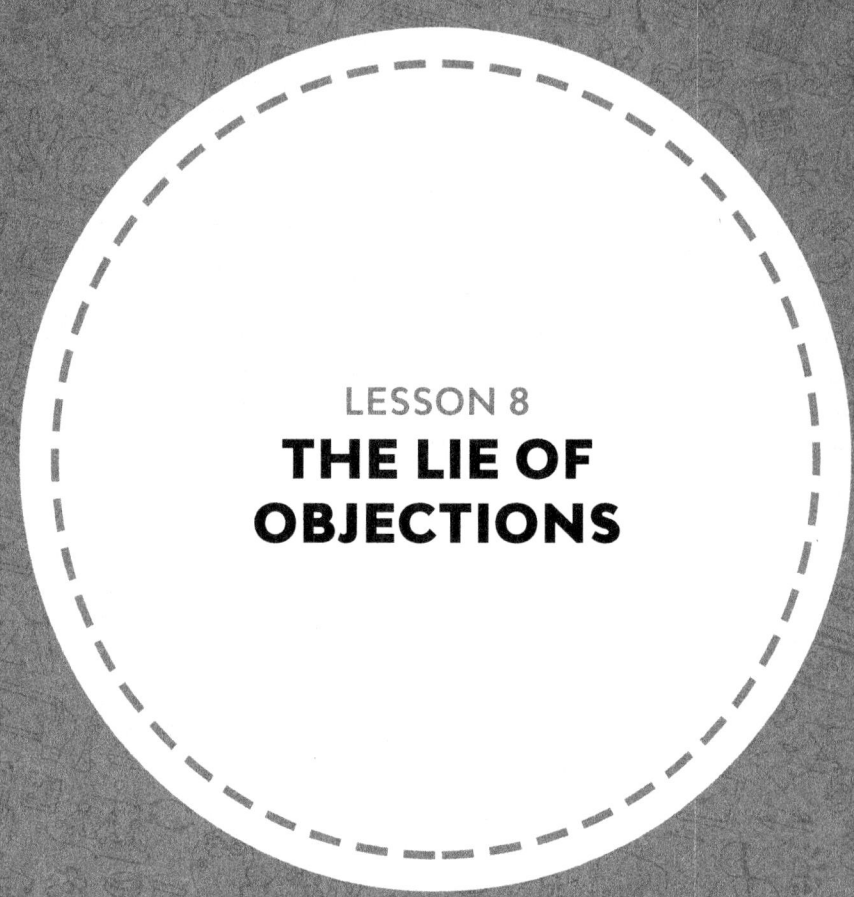

LESSON 8
THE LIE OF OBJECTIONS

LEAD YOUR TEAM!

Lesson 8
The Lie of Objections

You're going to hear lots of objections from candidates you approach about the business. Your first inclination is going to be to learn how to overcome every objection you hear. Usually, that is the wrong approach.

If you are receiving lots of objections, a better idea is to look at how you are presenting the opportunity to people. The presentations you give to people need to address the basic and frequent objections to what you are offering.

That means questions such as:

What about legality?
Do I have time?
Does the business really work?

… and other similar objections that shouldn't even come up. If they are, these objections aren't real but usually misdirection.

When your candidates voice objections, what they usually mean is "You haven't shown me how those great products and business opportunity apply to ME. You haven't demonstrated how this is relevant to MY life."

So stop looking for catchy comebacks to every objection. Instead, look at how you are presenting the opportunity.

Are you talking about features of your products or company? Candidates couldn't care less about that.

Your company is debt-free? No one cares.

Your sponsor makes $200,000 a month? No one cares.

Your CEO has a master's degree and is on the board of the DSA? No one cares.

Your company travels to Brazil to get a root to grind up as an ingredient in your energy drink? No one cares.

You pay 25 percent in the lesser leg, 20 percent matching bonus on personal enrollees, and have an infinity override for Diamond Directors? No one has any idea what that means. And no one cares.

You want to know the real objections you need to overcome? Your candidates need to know things like:

- Will I enjoy working with this person if they sponsor me?

- Will they help me?

- Do I feel like I belong here?

- Will these products add value to my life?

- How would I earn one of those bonus cars?

- Will my sponsor help me succeed?

- Are there tools and processes in place to help me do this

well?

- Is my sponsor just looking to make money off me or are they genuinely interested in my success?

- Are these people going somewhere I want to go and doing something I want to be a part of?

These are the real issues your candidates are concerned with. Make sure your sponsoring materials and process answer these questions and you will attract the right people for your team!

LESSON 9
IT'S NEVER ABOUT THE HYPE

LEAD YOUR TEAM!

Lesson 9
It's Never About the Hype

There was a post on Facebook the other day from a long-time "MLM Junkie" announcing that he was putting together his team to launch another company. He had five openings for leaders who would receive $50,000-a-month deals, and ten spots for people who would get $10,000-a-month deals.

I didn't know whether to laugh or cry…

Because this means there is another gullible owner of a new company who is going to piss away a couple million dollars to get this parasite and his cronies to launch his new company. And nine or ten months from now, this con artist and his merry band of mercenaries will move on to the next hot deal.

And, of course, there will be thousands of little people who jumped on board, getting no deals, thinking they were riding the next big wave. This happens so often it is unconscionable.

There is a large group of these whores selling themselves to the highest bidder, flitting from deal to deal. In some markets such as Australia for example, this is an epidemic. Every six months a new company opens there, waving around deals. The same cast of sorry characters jumps from the old to the new, and nothing permanent is ever built.

Many people who run legitimate companies see flaky start-ups poaching people with sweetheart deals and think they need to offer similar deals in order to compete.

Big mistake.

For the most part, the people attracted by these deals are mercenaries, with no loyalty to the company, products, or even their own team. And as soon as the payouts stop and they have to survive on their own business-building efforts, they're shopping for their next deal.

Of course in the meantime, they are pulling in gullible distributors by waving around their bonus checks and bragging on their earnings. But the average person has no shot at those incomes, unless they get the same sweetheart deal. Which they won't.

If you want to build a reputable company, you must first understand that real leaders can't be bought. On the surface, it looks like you are at an unfair advantage, because start up deals are able to steal away some of your people. But if you will resist the urge to compete in kind, you'll see these deals are usually gone within a year or two. The deals eventually run out and the people who got them are right behind.

Real leadership requires integrity. You need to be able to look a prospect in the eye and promise them they have the same opportunity you had. And you have to create it

Now I don't count other people's money and I won't say there is never a place for this. There are cases where a company is sold, goes out of business, or loses its way. Top people may find the only way they can keep their integrity is to leave.

Based upon a distributor's track record, a company may

choose to guarantee them a certain income while this person regroups and rebuilds. My comments to the companies on this would be:

Make sure the person you're giving the guarantee to has actually built something real and isn't one of the many whores out there ripping you off. And if you're a distributor who finds yourself in circumstances like this, don't mislead prospects about your income.

It's never about the hype and rah-rah. If your recruiting platform is about "catching the wave" or being the next "hot deal," you're building on sand.

> **You need to build on the rock-solid foundation of a strong customer base, duplicable system, competent leadership and impeccable integrity.**

The people you will attract because you have a yellow Lamborghini or wave around eight-foot-wide bonus checks are probably not the people who will build you an enduring business. If you're recruiting based on your results or the results of your top leaders, you're succumbing to hype.

Building a successful team – and demonstrating true leadership – is always about building people's belief that they can actually do the business successfully themselves and use the business as a platform to improve their lives. Do that and you'll build a truly great team.

LESSON 10
STOP LOOKING FOR OUTSIDE VALIDATION

LEAD YOUR TEAM!

Lesson 10
Stop Looking for Outside Validation

Want to build a remarkable business? It would help if you believed your business was amazing to begin with.

I'm old enough to remember when our profession was suspect, struggling for credibility, fighting for our right to exist.

We had to justify the business model and distinguish ourselves from the scams, pyramid schemes, and money games that came before us. (And will always be around in some fashion or another.) Every presentation and series of marketing materials had to explicitly explain the difference between a legitimate network marketing opportunity and an illegal plan.

Those days are long gone…

Today we have numerous direct selling, party plan, and network marketing companies that each produce at least a billion dollars a year in revenue. Some in multiples of that.

General awareness and acceptance of our profession has never been higher. We are frequently featured in those mainstream business publications. Our companies trade on the major stock exchanges. And unless you live in a cabin in the deep woods or on Antarctica, you've met someone who earns a five- or even six-figure monthly income in our business. Probably a few.

So why are so many people in our profession so insecure and desperate for validation? Why do they grasp at every innocuous mention of the business from any mainstream publication, breathlessly trumpet every pandering comment a motivational speaker makes about their company, and frantically seek endorsements from entrepreneurs in other sectors?

Yes, it's great that former president Bill Clinton spoke to the DSA and mentioned some positive things about our business. Lovely that authors like Robert Kiyosaki and David Bach support the business model in their books. Wonderful that Tony Robbins and Richard Branson have spoken positively about the profession from the stage.

But you can't get validation from any of those people. You have to bring your own.

I'm the middle child of three kids, raised by a single mother who supported us by knocking on doors selling AVON products. I was a teenage drug addict and alcoholic and made some very poor choices in my early years. I was expelled from high school and in jail by 15 years old.

There were no colleges offering me scholarships and no Fortune 500 companies recruiting me. I was scuffling along, trying to make my way in the world when I was presented the concept of network marketing and explained leverage for the first time.

Inherently I knew this was something big. I understood that

this was the missing element in my knowledge – how to escape the grind of trading hours for dollars and finding a way to actually break through and create a concrete and sustainable income.

Today I'm a wealthy man, living the life I have designed for myself. And I owe all that to this extraordinary, challenging and wonderful business model of network marketing and the leverage it offers.

I have sponsored men who didn't own a suit or tie and seen them grow into powerful executives. I've sponsored single mothers struggling to feed their family and watched them develop into powerful and successful role models for their children. I've seen people join the business desperate for cars, possessions and fame – and then learn the joys of contribution, service and giving.

I don't need anyone to validate the business for me. I know why the business is amazing. And you need to know this too.

You have to know. And know that you know. Only then will you inspire candidates and team members that you are going somewhere, and they'll want to go there with you.

The network marketing business isn't easy. We don't have a boss that gives us a raise and often don't even have a sponsor who will give us praise. We have to summon the courage to pick up the phone and call prospects. We have to get into the car and drive to homes of people we don't know. We have to take long plane rides to work with long-distance lines. And maybe worst of all, we have to face our fears…

Fear of rejection, fear of failure, even fear of success. But we do it. Every week.

We look for support where we can, feed our minds with positive programming, and hang around positive people. But when it's time to pick up the phone, it's only you. Which is why we need the most important thing:

Self-belief.

You have to have self-validation and self-reinforcement. No one can do that for you. Outside sources can inspire you, but only you can motivate you.

You have to be your biggest fan. Boom the boom sticks, wave the terrible towels, wear the rally caps, or any of the other crazy things sports fans do to cheer on their favorite teams and athletes. You have to cheer on you.

So when it comes to crunch time, please remember a couple things…

The work you do matters. It matters to you, because you're building self-discipline. You're developing character and new skills that will help you in all areas of your life, both professional and personal. It matters because you care enough about yourself to challenge yourself, to refuse mediocrity and go after what you want in life.

It matters to the people you bring into your business. The customers who are helped by your products and the team members who are building their dreams. They won't all lose

80 pounds, look like Miss America or cure an incurable disease. They won't all drive bonus cars, cash huge bonus checks, or become millionaires. But their lives will be better, because you gave them the opportunity.

You give people their dreams back. And that is not an insignificant thing. Even better, you give them a vehicle to go after those dreams.

Whether they want freedom or security, a new Lamborghini or to build an orphanage – you give them a real shot at doing that. And that's why you're special. That's why you're amazing. Because you're not only a dreamer, you're a doer. An entrepreneur, and entrepreneurs are the people who drive the free enterprise system, create innovations, build value, and create wealth.

So take a minute today, glance at your dream board and remember why you do what you do. Then get in front of a mirror, look yourself in the eye, and say, "Congratulations. Thanks for being amazing."

LESSON 11
YOUR BEST INVESTMENT

LEAD YOUR TEAM!

Lesson 11
Your Best Investment

Every few weeks I get a similar message. Someone has a brilliant idea for a new business venture and they are offering the amazing opportunity to be the sole investor. I check it out and can usually pass it up after a cursory look. The reason is the person bringing me the idea isn't even invested in it. Mentally, physically, or financially.

In other words, they think they might have an idea they believe in, but they don't want to commit to it. They are hoping I will commit to it and then they'll know if it is viable.

If you want someone to invest in your idea, project or business, you better be the number one investor, all in, frothing at the mouth to make it a reality. Otherwise you're just a tourist.

Think about how many people approach their network marketing business. Most treat it like an occasional hobby. Think about how you approach your network marketing business. This is your future we're talking about. Are you investing in that future? Are you investing in yourself?

Let's explore what that looks like in our profession. The first and most important investment is in yourself – meaning your personal growth, self-development, and learning new skillsets.

Your business will grow only as fast as you do.

This begins with your library. True leaders are always learning, so they're forever adding to their collection of cherished books, audios, and videos. Make sure you are working on you, every single day, through outside resources.

The next and natural extension of that development is attending events. Every year schedule some time and resources to attend one or two seminars or workshops outside the business, just focusing on your growth as a person. Something that nourishes your mind, body and soul.

If you have something ongoing in personal growth, that is a big plus. Learn a foreign language, take yoga or meditation classes, or join a book club or study group. Iron sharpens iron, so put yourself in environments that challenge you and force you to grow.

Then, it's very important to attend the major events put on by your sponsorship line and company. They are the glue that holds your team, and thus your business, together.

I recently received an email from a guy who dropped out of my business after two months. Why did he quit?

He said he didn't have money to even buy the product. Now, of course, he has what most people would consider a real job and earns decent money by conventional standards. It wasn't that he didn't have money. The truth is, buying the product wasn't a priority for him.

If you asked me the real reason he dropped out, I would say it's because he never attended a major function. And we had one his second month in the business. But no matter how hard I pushed, he cried poor and wouldn't go. And if I've learned anything, it is this:

People who don't attend functions are at serious risk to drop out. If they aren't building their belief at these events, it becomes just too easy to quit.

New recruits desperately need the major events to develop skills, build dreams, create confidence, develop goals, meet successful people, and create game plans. Not to mention another 50 reasons we don't have time to talk about now. But, despite having a steady job and good income, this guy insisted he couldn't afford paying $100 – the price of a dinner for two at a nice restaurant – to attend an event that would help him develop his business.

So back to the email…

He was sending it from the Dominican Republic, where he had travelled to attend a circuit party. For two weeks.

Like a lot of people, he'll have a week or two of fun once a year, then scrimp for the other 50. I hope he has a wonderful time. But it's too bad that when he gets back he'll have to economize for the next year and play the same scene all over again.

To have success in our business you have to attend the major events. And you have to create a culture that encourages, even mandates that your team attends them.

There are five reasons we conduct major events. And everyone – and I do mean everyone – is always in need of one of those five things.

The Five Reasons for Major Events:
1) Gain knowledge
2) Improve attitude
3) Change behavior
4) Develop skills
5) Build belief

Every time there is a major event coming up, one of those five things is the most important outcome for you. So invest in yourself and get there.

Finally, the other investment I want to encourage you to make is the one of building long-distance lines. This is a great investment for your business because it diversifies and protects your income. If your organization is in different states or countries, developing long-distance lines protects you against economic downturns, natural disasters, negative publicity, loss of a leader and other challenges. Diversifying your group geographically gives you more security.

If you want to be the leader of a large team and create solid growth in your network, be the first one to drive the miles. Because that's how organizations grow.

It starts with someone with a dream. Then you attract others who also have a dream. Next it begins to spread. At this point you need to taproot down the lines. And this means you're driving two, three, maybe even four hours away, helping new people with home presentations. It may mean driving eight or ten hours once a month to work with a long-distance line or attend a function. Pretty soon this will mean jumping on a plane.

Every month I look in my back office and to see where I have fires developing. Then I hop on a plane and go pour gasoline on the fires.

If you're committed to becoming a leader, you should be traveling at least a day or two a month, tap-rooting down the group. A mid level rank should be out four or five days a months. And a top rank may be traveling seven to ten days a month.

If you are just starting out, even the first level of one or two days a month is going to be a challenge, because you've got a day job you need to report to. But if your goal is to leave your day job, you need to make that investment and sacrifice at some point.

There are general guidelines of course, so check with your sponsorship line. But make sure that every month you are investing in some long-distance lines.

LESSON 12
PRESENT AN EMPOWERING STORY

LEAD YOUR TEAM!

Lesson 12
Present an Empowering Story

Okay, you earned a free bonus car. Your mother is proud of you. But we don't really care.

Because it's not about your car. It's what your car can mean to the rest of your team.

And the same is true for that luxury cruise you won, the big bonus checks you're cashing, and the $50,000 watch you're wearing.

Contrary to popular belief, nobody on your team is going to build better or bigger because you got a snazzy new Philippe Patek. In fact, a lot of times all the check waving and rah-rah actually un-inspires people.

Here's why...

No one wants to hear how rich, sexy, amazing, and happy you are. Or at least they don't until after they heard how poor, unattractive, mediocre, and miserable you used to be.

It seems everyone is trained to tell their story in network marketing. Boast about all the bling, bonuses, and big bucks they made. But that doesn't inspire people. Remember this:

The only reason you tell your story is for the lesson or inspiration it holds for the audience. Anything else is just beating your chest.

I sat through a convention where speaker after speaker told their story to "motivate" the audience. It was like they all used the same PowerPoint template.

First were their baby pictures, then those from childhood. The house they grew up in. Then came their teen years. Their first beat-up car and the simple apartment they moved into after college. The guys showed their sports pictures, the gals showed their high school yearbooks. This went on for half an hour each.

If you're not Lady Gaga or Pitbull, we don't want to know that much about you!

Your story is inspiring only if it teaches us that you have faced some of the challenges, obstacles and adversity we are facing. And the fact that you persevered inspires us to know that we too can persevere.

Like authors or motivational speakers, we don't tell our story because people are interested in our story. We tell our story because of the impact it can have on the audience.

So the first step in moving from an excited distributor to a leader who can motivate your team is to be able to tell your story in an inspiring way. And do so from the perspective of the prospect.

So how do you do that?

Be vulnerable. Be empathetic. And most of all, be authentic. You don't have to have an "I used to sleep under a bridge" story. (Unless you really did.) But you do need a story that reveals some of the challenges you faced. The fears you overcame. The sacrifices you were willing to make, to reach the success you have achieved.

Follow this simple formula, whether you're doing a 30-second testimonial or a 60-minute keynote about your journey.

1. Tell us what you do (or used to do) before network marketing.
2. Tell us the problem with what you do (or used to do).
3. Tell us how network marketing is solving or has solved that problem.

Examples:

My name is Mary Smith and I'm a nurse. The problem with that is the job is high stress and low pay. I joined network marketing because it's low stress and offers unlimited income.

My name is Ronnie Jones. I'm a long-haul trucker and that takes me away from my family for long periods of time. I joined the business so I can be there when my kids get home from school.

The whole idea is that there will be people in the audience who relate to your story. They are facing the challenges you speak about and the inspiration comes from realizing they now have a possible solution to eliminate these challenges.

If you're just talking about your cars, watches, and trips, the candidates in the audience are thinking, "What an arrogant jerk. He doesn't know anything about me. Why is he throwing all his money and success in my face?"

Not a very good strategy for winning converts. Here's what you need the candidates in the audience to be thinking…

"Wow. She has been exactly where I am now. She faced down some of the fears I have and has overcome some of the challenges I am currently facing. She is qualified to lead me. And I want to follow her."

And when that happens, you are on your way to becoming a leader in our profession.

LESSON 13
BUILD TO CRITICAL MASS

LEAD YOUR TEAM!

Lesson 13
Build to Critical Mass

Whatever you do, don't fall prey to believing the title that your comp plan gives you! Know this: Companies like to create titles that sound important. But you shouldn't take them so literally.

You enroll two people and they call you a "Supervisor," so you think you're supposed to stop sponsoring people and supervise the two you have. If you enroll four, they call you something like "Manager," so you stop recruiting to instead manage the team. Or you break "Director," so you think your job is to direct the team.

Let's get something clear…

When you have a team of at least 10,000 members, then you can start to think about supervising, managing or directing it. Until then, keep enrolling!

We can also make the argument that you shouldn't ever stop enrolling, just reduce it proportionately. I was still enrolling even when my last team had more than 200,000 members.

Why would I? Why should you?

The opportunities available for your prospects aren't any less desirable simply because you have a large team. In fact, they're probably better. And you will always be encountering new people who could use what you have to offer. So please don't freeze anyone out.

The other consideration is the surprising reality that it is actually easier to grow the business fast than it is to grow it slow. Seriously.

There is a special excitement palpable in teams that are growing fast. People sense it, feel it and are emboldened by it. When they see new team members under them in their back office it creates real excitement. Watching meetings, conference calls and webcasts grow in size creates the same kind of excitement. And there is also a healthy, sibling rivalry type of enthusiasm created.

Another factor is the initial fervor, zeal, and passion most people begin the venture with. For most, their excitement and enthusiasm will never be higher than during this beginning stage. So if you go all out, many of them will follow your suit, creating an even more powerful energy and momentum for the entire team.

That excitement and enthusiasm causes everyone to reach higher, try harder and stay more focused. Compare that with the alternate possibility…

How excited do you think someone gets from their organization growing from ten people in January to 11 in February? What happens to energy in meetings that have plateaued at the same attendance for the last year? How do your people respond when they hear about teams from other companies creating strong momentum while they are stuck in neutral?

If you are building your business slowly and deliberately, you are doing the job the hardest way possible.

So give yourself a break. Keep sponsoring strong when you first begin the business. (Or start sponsoring strong, if you started out slow and you're just waking up now as you read this!) When you enroll a large number of people, you create that sibling rivalry we discussed, which helps drive most of the team.

You're also doing one of the most important roles of a leader: modeling the correct behavior for your team to follow. You provide every single person on your team with a better chance of reaching success by demonstrating the best path to follow.

LESSON 14
BECOME AMAZING AT MEETING PEOPLE

LEAD YOUR TEAM!

Lesson 14
Become Amazing at Meeting People

Everyone comes into the business with their current list – the people they know. And how you do with that list depends on what your relationships with those people have been up to that point.

Some people start with a list of 25 and get in 18. Others start with a list of 200 and can't get in eight. And it's really not their invitation skills. It's how they interacted with that list before they ever joined the business. That's the good news and the bad news.

When I started in network marketing, my list did nothing for me. Why? Because I wasn't very well liked. The interactions I had been having with people weren't pleasant for them, and the last thing they wanted was to have to spend more time with me.

I had no credibility or trust in the business, because people didn't like or trust me before I joined the business!

You and everyone you bring into the business will face the same dynamic. Your early success is going to be determined by the level of relationships and influence you had before you even joined.

After being out of the business for a few years, I got back

into the game. My list of contacts worked amazingly well for me! What changed?

I had. I had become a better person and thus inspired belief and trust in the people around me. My relationships with people were built on mutual respect and value.

This is the reality for everyone entering the business. How you've been with people in the past will impact how well your invitations work with them when you begin. For some of you, like me, you'll need the personal growth that comes from the business in order to do well from your first list. You may actually do better with the new people you meet because you can start fresh.

It is one of the reasons that using third party tools is so important. These tools make the process about the opportunity, instead of being about you. This situation also reinforces why the skillset of meeting people is such an important dynamic in the business. Even though I had good relationships the second time around, I still needed to meet new people. And so do you.

I've earned more than $11 million since I got back in the biz. And more than half of that is from volume produced by people I didn't know when I got in. And every top leader you talk to will tell you a similar story.

A huge part of your income will come from people you don't know yet when you begin the business. Meeting people is a skill, and one that anyone can develop. And that skill separates the amateurs from the professionals. Professionals don't complain about what they can't do. They learn how to do it.

Amateurs say, "I don't know that many people" or "I've already talked with everyone on my list." Professionals recognize that meeting people is a skill, and they practice it continuously to get better at it.

Some important points to remember:
- In the beginning, you will pay or you will get paid for who you were before you joined the business.
- The good prospects aren't in your home. The people who live there are either already in or aren't good prospects.
- Get through your first list as quick as possible and learn how to meet new people.
- Your candidate list should be organic, always changing as people join or opt out and you meet new ones.
- The best time to meet new people is before you get through your first list.
- You can always change your situation by going out and meeting some new people today!

LESSON 15
BECOME BEYOND AMAZING AT INVITING

LEAD YOUR TEAM!

Lesson 15
Become Beyond Amazing at Inviting

If there were only one skill you could focus on getting better at, it would have to be inviting. That's because having good invitation skills can make you rich and successful faster than almost anything else.

Think about it: Inviting is the nexus of our business. We invite people to review DVDs, watch webcasts, get on conference calls, and attend meetings. Almost nothing of consequence happens in the recruiting process that doesn't hinge on the invitation.

The most critical part of any recruiting process is the invitation.
You want your invitations to be as powerful, compelling, and intriguing as possible. So to make yours as effective, let me share my...

Top Ten Keys to Powerful Inviting

1) Do your inviting over the phone.
Never do invites in person because that encourages candidates to interrogate you with question after question. The goal here is not to get people in the business or even make a presentation. Your goal with the invitation is simply to confirm an appointment where they can see the presentation.
Often if you do invitations in person, the candidate will try to badger you into explaining the whole business opportunity

on the spot. This almost guarantees a poor result. So always do your inviting on the phone.

2) Get off the phone within two minutes.
Get on, get off. In two minutes or less. Simply doing this will dramatically raise your compliance rates and the number of people who actually show up for a presentation. And the more people you get to an actual presentation, the more you'll bring into the business. It's that simple.

This way, you can actually start your calls with the question, "You got two minutes?" Which then sets you up to be off the phone in that time. When people press you with question after question, you can reply with something like "I can't do business on the phone" or "There's a presentation you need to see in person." This response avoids your getting dragged into endless questions, and allows you to make a lot more invitations in less time. Remember, every second you are on the line after two minutes decreases your positive results.

3) Have your dream board in front of you while inviting.
A huge but unseen part of inviting is the energy, passion, and intensity you bring to that invitation. It's very important that you get on these calls with a high level of energy. The best way to do that is to stay focused on why you're doing the business in the first place.

So take a minute to look it over before you start. Look at all of the things you want to do, have, and become in your life. And think about how advancing your business will contribute to making those goals, dreams, and desires a reality. This will keep your passion high during your calls.

4) Focus only on the desired outcome, which is to get their agreement to see a presentation.
It's easy to be distracted and think your job is to get a customer or new distributor. But those objectives come later. The purpose of the invite call – and the only purpose – is to get an appointment where the candidate will view a presentation, whether in person or online. So keep your focus on that outcome and don't let anything take you off track.

5) Invite both spouses to the presentation.
If your candidate is married, be sure to invite their spouse as well. If you present just to one, that person must go back home and try to excite the other half. That creates a large drop-off in results. So do your best to get both partners there.

6) If you are booking a one-on-one or two-on-one, book it at their home.
This is a position on which I've evolved over time. Initially I always chose a neutral location like a coffee shop. But that was very depressing with a lot of no shows. When I switched to going to their homes, my results went up. More than a couple times, the people had completely forgot about the appointment. But because they were home anyway, the presentation went forward.

7) Repeat the appointment at the end of the call.
At the very last part of the call, make sure to repeat the day, time, and place of the appointment to anchor it in their mind

and confirm you both are in sync.

8) Don't call to reconfirm.

This is another position on which I have changed over the years. Earlier in my career, I always called back close to the appointment to reconfirm. However, I find most people are so distracted and disorganized they use the confirmation call to cancel. So now I never call back to reconfirm. I either do nothing or text when I'm on the way. Something like "OMW, see you in 20."

9) Set aside a block of time exclusively for inviting, and make as many invitations as you can fit in that time.

If you're always multi-tasking, inviting has a way of getting pushed to the bottom of the priority list. So set aside a specific block of time during which you invite people to a group presentation (group, in-home, or online).

You want to be able to set aside 30 to 45 minutes for uninterrupted invitation calls and get in at least 20 to 30. This way you're not invested in everyone saying yes. You're making enough invites to get some serious traction for your event. If you do 60 or 90, you'll have dramatically higher numbers and much better attendance at your event.

10) Always answer a question with another question.

You're looking for people who are looking. So it's not about selling, begging or convincing. When you make a call, go into a "three strikes and you're out" mindset – meaning that you won't go further than three questions to persuade the person you called.

Someone who is definitely looking will say yes. If so, confirm the place and time and get off the phone. Make your next call while you're hot. However, most people will try to start the interrogation here. They say:

What is it?

Is it Amway?

Is this one of those things?

What kind of business is it?

That's strike one. And no matter what they say, you respond with a question: *"Have you read any of Robert Kiyosaki's Rich Dad, Poor Dad books? It will make more sense when you see the presentation. Can you come?"*

If they say yes, confirm the place and time and get off the phone. Make your next call while you're hot.

Some will still ask questions:

What is it?

Is it Amway?

Is this one of those things?

What kind of business is it?

That's strike two. And no matter what they say, you respond with a question: *"Have you read any of Randy Gage's prosperity books? It will make more sense when you see the presentation. Can you come?"*

If they say yes, confirm the place and time and get off the phone. Make your next call while you're hot.

If they say no or ask more questions again, that's strike three. You say, *"Doesn't sound like you're looking right now, so let's forget it. Let me know if you change your mind."*

Then get off the phone and on to your next call. Don't beg, don't bargain, don't diminish the opportunity. If they're not looking, you're not looking for them. For some people, this "takeaway" is what actually gets them to say yes.

Following these guidelines will dramatically improve your attendance and eventual enrollment success. Always do your invites with passion, intensity, and urgency. Look for the people who respond to your excitement and lock down that appointment. Get off the phone quickly with those who don't. Then jump on the next call…

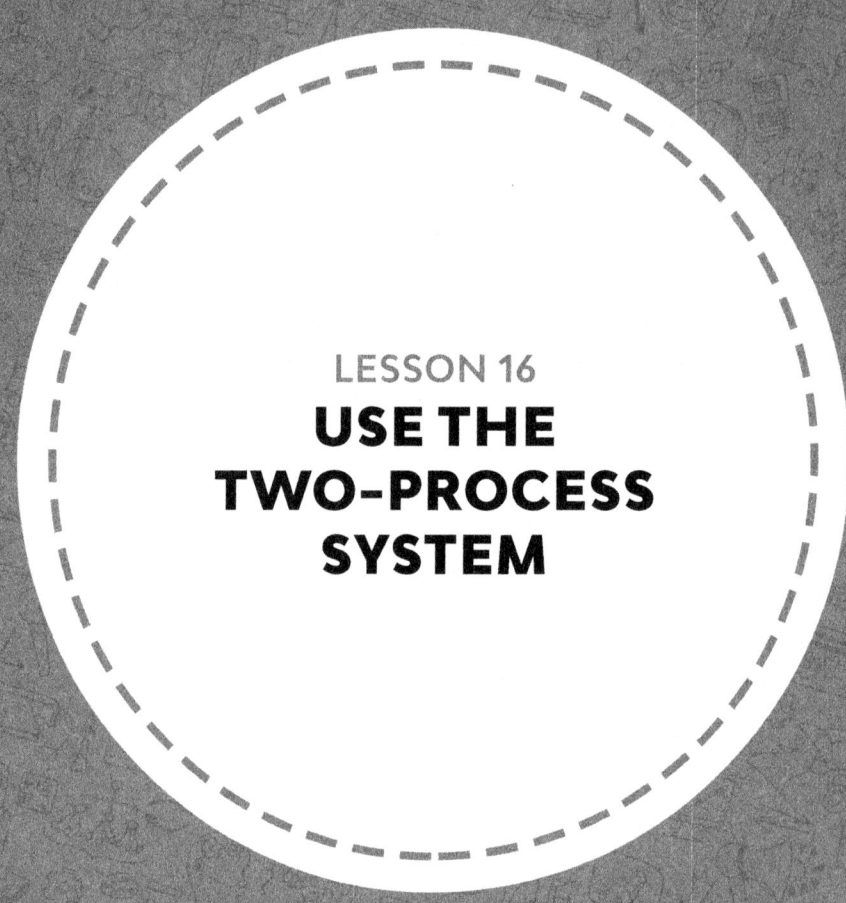

LESSON 16
USE THE TWO-PROCESS SYSTEM

LEAD YOUR TEAM!

Lesson 16
Use the Two-Process System

This is one of the most important lessons you will ever learn in building a large team. And it is shocking how few leaders understand it. Which explains why there are so many "grinders" in our business – people who are overwhelmed each day, trying to keep up with all the demands on their time.

They fall into a pattern as to how they work with their personal enrollees. But this neglects a vital fact about the business. Not everyone you sponsor is going to work and produce at the same levels. And in fact, there will be a huge disparity between the players and the tourists. If you try to work with each person the same way, you will be wasting lots of time with people not deserving of your attention and, conversely, neglecting some serious people who need more of your support. If I have learned anything in business, in relationships, in life – it is this:

Don't disburse your relationship energy on a "first come, first served" basis. Be mindful of who you are spending time with.

The way to apply this philosophy to your team building is by creating two categories for the people you work with.

Category one is the people who may talk a great game but don't actually do anything. Or they are people who are always threatening to go to work, but they want you to change the comp plan, fix the economy or develop a new product line first.

Because they don't actually want to build anything, they have lots of free time and will demand constant audiences with you. They like to make two-hour-long phone or Skype calls complaining about everything they believe needs to be changed. They are energy vampires, so they are always the squeaky wheel, vying for your attention.

You simply can't have enough time for people like this, and they are a very bad investment of this precious resource. So it's necessary to move them into the "group attention" category.

Every time you are hit on by people in this category, you direct them to the next webcast, appropriate training video or article, or next live event. Send them to the resources that address whatever their request is, but limit the personal interaction you have with them.

This frees you up to work with the players. These are the people who really want success, really want to work for it, and just sincerely need guidance or mentoring on how they can be more effective.

These are the people you counsel with, fly to their markets to do events, and just all-around invest in developing their skills, providing guidance and building their belief and confidence. This is the greatest investment you will ever make in your business – investing in your future leaders.

LESSON 17
SOLVE PROBLEMS

LEAD YOUR TEAM!

Lesson 17
Solve Problems

BREAKING NEWS: There are going to be challenges when you build your business. People will make mistakes. Your team leaders will experiment with many approaches. Some will work great. Others not so great.

The company will have missteps along the way. That's because there are no perfect companies – only companies that are perfect for you. So let's lose the notion that everything will work out perfectly, flawlessly, and harmoniously. You're going to face challenging issues.

The fascinating thing is how many people believe the way to demonstrate their leadership capabilities is to create laundry lists of everything that is wrong with the team system, the company, or the profession.

Anybody can point out problems. If you want to lead and inspire a large team, you need to provide solutions.

Don't send your sponsor a frantic text telling them there are four typos in the new product catalog. Send them a PDF with the errors highlighted and the correct copy written in, so they can immediately forward it to someone who can fix it.

Don't call your sponsor to say you think the team website sucks. Send a thoughtful email with suggestions on how to make it better.

Don't bitch because the company doesn't have buses running between the host hotel and the convention venue. Gather some of your people, book an UBER XL and get it done.

Victims can tell you what the problems are. Victors can tell you what the solutions are. You can be a victim or you can be a victor, but you can't be both. Choose wisely.

LESSON 18
KILL DISTRACTIONS!

LEAD YOUR TEAM!

Lesson 18
Kill Distractions!

If you want to be a leader in our profession and build a large team, you have to kill distractions. Relentlessly.

Because as your organization grows, so will the possible distractions. And make no mistake – everything that doesn't produce new customers and grow the team is a distraction. And you have to kill them.

Every team member you have faces a huge decision, each and every day. They have to decide should they pick up the phone and prospect a candidate – facing the possibility of rejection – or can they find a distraction and practice avoidance behavior?

Your company just introduced a new protein shake in six delicious flavors. Know what your new distributor will ask? "When will they have mango flavor?"

That's a distraction. Kill it.

You just sponsored a new distributor in Kansas. Know what she will say when you get her started? "My sister lives in Nigeria. When is the company going to open there?"

That's a distraction. Kill it.

Your team members will suggest that if the company pays more money in the comp plan they can grow faster.

That's a distraction. Kill it.

We don't control the wind. We control only what direction we can turn the sail.

As distributors, we don't develop products, design IT, create the compensation plan, manage the warehouse, create the company logo, or hire the customer service employees. We don't control elections, public policy, the weather or the economy. All those things are distractions. You kill them – or they kill your business.

We present the business opportunity and get customers. That's how we get paid. Everything else is a distraction.

Every time you have a team member who becomes seduced by a distraction, you have to kill it and get them focused on building their customer base and getting prospects in front of a presentation.

Team members get distracted. Team leaders kill distractions. Which one will you be?

So when Lourdes says, "There is a new company starting and I hear they pay an extra 1 percent of the breakaway volume for the third generation."

You say, "Lourdes, that's a distraction. Let's focus on what you can control. Let's get out your candidate list and start inviting people to the next presentation."

When David says, "I heard that Jimmy, one of our top leaders, just left and went to a competing company. Is that true? Why did he leave?"

You say, "David, that's a distraction. Let's focus on what you can control. We wish Jimmy the best of success for his future. Let's get out your candidate list and start inviting people to the next presentation."

When Rebecca says, "How will the UK leaving the EU affect the price of herbs in the South American rainforest, which would impact the exchange rate for the commissions we get paid?"

You say, "Rebecca, that's a distraction. Let's focus on what you can control. Let's get out your candidate list and start inviting people to the next presentation."

Know what you can control and what you can't. And remember that every moment you spend on something you can't control is stolen from something you can.

LESSON 19
OWN THE STAGE

LEAD YOUR TEAM!

Lesson 19
Own the Stage

If I wake you up at 3 am, shine a flashlight in your face, and ask you to do a 30-minute training on inviting skills – could you do it?
If you plan on being a leader, the answer better be "Yes."

Because your ability as a trainer plays a pivotal role in your success as a network marketing leader. Because every leader needs to be able to conduct a training segment on any one of five topic areas – at any time.

These areas are:
- Meeting People
- Working a Candidate List
- Inviting
- Follow-Up
- Your Product Line

If you've followed my work for any length of time, you know I consider the first four points to be the basic skill sets that everyone must master. And the fifth topic is necessary education that every leader should be able to impart. Being able to train in these five topics are the "table stakes" – meaning the minimum requirement of skill for a serious leader.

You should be able to conduct a 15-, 30-, 60-, or 90-minute version of every one of these. (At any time.) You expand each segment as needed by adding in additional stories, jokes, examples, case studies, role-playing, or other audience participation.

So let's suppose you arrive at a major event thinking you are not on the agenda. The event organizer informs you that one of the scheduled trainers has missed a flight connection, and they need you to take that presenter's place.

You shouldn't fall into a panic or mutter about not having a PowerPoint presentation prepared. The only correct response is "Certainly. I'd be happy to help. What's the topic and how long do you need?"

By the way, here's a different, but related scenario...

Let's suppose you come to an event prepared to give a 90-minute presentation, but the event is running 30 minutes behind. Your job as a leader is to do an amazing 60-minute presentation on the topic and get the event back on time. This is what makes you a professional.

LESSON 20
THE CHALLENGES ON YOUR PATH... ARE THE PATH

LEAD YOUR TEAM!

Lesson 20
The Challenges on Your Path... Are the Path

It took me more than twenty years of intense self-development study to understand the single most basic concept in self-development...

You don't conquer enough challenges to achieve some idealized existence where there are no more challenges. You overcome challenges to prepare for the next, greater challenge.

I had always thought that if I did enough personal growth and self-development I would reach some type of nirvana state – some plane of existence where discord, problems and relationship issues no longer existed. A place only of honeydew and rainbows, moonbeams and unicorns.

When I discovered that overcoming a challenge simply led me to the next, bigger challenge, what a letdown that was! Or at least that's what I thought initially. But my real breakthrough came when I realized these challenges were a gift to me.

Challenges are the stepping stones that allow us to become better leaders, create stronger teams, and do things that make a true difference.

No one wants to learn from the person who has never held

a secret meeting, been rejected, or had a key person drop out. You earned those scars. Be proud of them. And allow them to serve their purpose.

Let your setbacks become the fuel that powers your greatest accomplishments. Learn the lessons and grow from them. Then teach those lessons to the people who need them.

LESSON 21
FIRE YOURSELF

LEAD YOUR TEAM!

Lesson 21
Fire Yourself

We talk a lot about leadership in this business. Everyone likes to believe they are a leader and that every new distributor they enroll is another leader. But are they really? Are you?

I have a pretty simple criteria I use to determine this: If the way you live and work your business inspires others to dream bigger, strive to accomplish more, and endeavor to become more – you are a leader.

People ask me for advice all the time on how to be a better leader. That advice is pretty simple. Stop aspiring to be a leader, stop training to become a leader, stop asking questions about becoming a leader, and start leading. If someone starts to follow you, you are a leader.

Lead like you don't have the rent and the landlord is coming tomorrow. Lead like your prospects don't have the rent and the landlord is coming tomorrow.

Lead like your products are amazing and people really need them. Lead like your prospects have mortgages, car payments, and credit card debt and are looking for a way out.

Please. Lead like you really believe in the business, your company and your products. Lead like you believe in the power of people. Just lead.

And once you become a great leader, fire

yourself.

Let me break all this down into its most elegant, straightforward, and clear interpretation. Your job is to work yourself out of a job.

The best leaders in network marketing are always developing new leaders. This is not a buzz phrase or a cliché. What we're talking about is a very real and very conscious decision to take regular action that fosters leadership development in your team.

Here's what that looks like:
Leaders don't make themselves indispensable.

Leave that crap for the corporate world. In our space, the best leaders make themselves replaceable. That means they are not the only ones who do all the presentations or training, creating everything, and deciding everything. They are always involving new team members – at a level commensurate to their skill level – to become part of these processes.

Leaders don't suck all of the oxygen from the room.

It's never all about them. They're always happy to see their team members shine and receive recognition and credit for their accomplishments.

Leaders recognize developing talent in people – often before they know it themselves.

So they are always surveying down through the group, scouting for people with drive and determination. And when they discover those qualities, they let these people know they are capable of team leadership. By doing this, they always have the next generation of leaders working their way up through the organization.

Most importantly, true leaders create a leadership factory in their organization.

They build an environment that fosters, nurtures and encourages leadership development for all those wanting to do that. This is one of those culture things and maybe the most important one in terms of developing strong, ongoing growth for your team.

Here are seven elements in the environment that will foster leadership development among the team:

1. The focus is forward. You can't live on ranks people broke three years ago. Learn from the lessons of the past. But keep the focus on the future, what people can do next, and where they want to go.

2. Diversity is celebrated. Yes, you should have a system and standardized processes. Certainly you want a team culture. But if you build that culture around external factors like dress codes, or religion, you will be excluding some great talent. Make your culture inclusive, not exclusive.

3. Pack leaders set the pace. One of the most beneficial things any organization can provide its members is to have people on the front line, leading the charge. The best way for someone to develop – in any area – is to have a talented person in front of them, leading the way, demonstrating what is possible. You need leaders rank advancing themselves, modeling the behavior that produces success.

4. The atmosphere is affirming. The world is filled with critics, naysayers and negative people. Your team doesn't need more negative messaging from their work with you. Make sure the environment is always encouraging, optimistic, and relentlessly positive.

5. Rank advancement is celebrated. Make sure your organization celebrates and recognizes achievements, growth and development.

6. Challenge is baked in the cake. Here's where you need to do something counterintuitive. People join organizations to feel comfortable. But the great organizations lure them out of their comfort zone and into the challenge zone. You don't want a team where people can simply phone in their participation. You want one that keeps them a little breathless to keep up.

7. The leadership path is designated. A very important element in the development of leaders is that people know what leadership in your organization looks like and the path that takes them there. There will be certain tasks, and roles that make up this path. It needs to be clear what these are so people who are interested can follow the track.

Now it should go without saying – but since you know me by now, you know it won't – that for you to create an environment that challenges people to grow, YOU need to be in one yourself. What does that look like?

You should wake up each day excited. Your team is growing. You are growing. You're being challenged enough so that you are out of your comfort zone frequently. You go all in, full out and play big. But you also eat well, sleep enough and rejuvenate yourself, so you're operating at a healthy peak state for extended levels. And the actions you take each day are congruent with who you are, who you want to become, and take you closer to where you want to be.

If you're not in that state right now, I want to help you. I offer my <u>Breakthrough U</u> Coaching Program. This is a very special program where I can work with you personally, helping you become the greatest leader you are capable of being. If that sounds intriguing, click the link above for the details. It's always an honor and a joy to walk across that stage and be presented with a pin signifying your next rank advancement. But that is mightily dwarfed by the much greater honor and joy to be watching as your team members walk across that stage.

True leadership is never about how many followers you have. It's about how many leaders you are developing.

So stop trying to be the superhero. Get rid of the cape and tights. This was never really about you anyway. It's about the people you can touch.

The people you can guide along the way. Step into their world and help them discover who they are really meant to be. The dreams they can achieve and the lives they can live. Become the leader they need – so they can become the leader they are meant to be.

Lead Your Team
Final Thoughts

We live in the most exciting time in human history. The speed of advances in areas like technology, wellness, longevity, medicine, manufacturing, social media, etc... is mind-boggling.

These advances are each creating new challenges in their own way. And each one of those challenges is a new opportunity for you and me and this amazing profession of direct selling.

In our profession, as in all professions, our success or failure will depend on the leadership we demonstrate. (Or don't.)

I believe our future is going to be brilliant. We're in a profession that operates by the prosperity principles of solving problems, adding value, and envisioning possibilities. So we have an opportunity to improve the world. And because we have that opportunity, we have that responsibility.

I'm up for the challenge. And my most fervent wish is that you are too!

RECOMMENDED RESOURCES
TAKE ADVANTAGE OF RANDY'S BUSINESS BUILDING RESOURCES

Visit NetworkMarketingTimes.com
for the latest resources and best prices!

CONNECT WITH RANDY GAGE

THE ULTIMATE LEADERSHIP TRAINING
MULTI-LEVEL MAYHEM

Multi-Level Mayhem

Mayhem is a high-level training on the concepts of leadership – and specifically how they apply in the network marketing and direct selling arena. Most particularly, the focus is on how these concepts play out in the process of team building.

It's a critical thinker's view on how you combine duplicable systems and structure, leadership development, and organizational culture to create powerful and sustained exponential growth.

Visit MultiLevelMarketing.com

THE FOUNDATION FOR DUPLICATION

MAKING THE FIRST CIRCLE WORK

Making the First Circle Work

This powerful little book from Randy Gage is exactly what you need to get duplication really happening throughout your organization.

Visit NetworkMarketingTimes.com

THE SCIENCE OF NETWORK MARKETING

HOW TO BUILD A MULTI-LEVEL MONEY MACHINE

How to Build a Multi-Level Money Machine

This book will teach you the science of Network Marketing. You'll learn the proven and predictable methods of operation to create real duplication on your team and develop true residual income – your own multi-level money machine! Order your copy now.

Visit NetworkMarketingTimes.com

GET STARTED IN NETWORK MARKETING
FIRST STEPS

First Steps

This successful 28-page booklet is perfect to start your new distributors on the right track. You make or break your new distributors in the first two weeks -- and the first 48 hours are critical. Get this booklet and insure your success.

Visit NetworkMarketingTimes.com

A MANIFESTO FOR ENTREPRENEURS

MAD GENIUS

Mad Genius

A unique book for entrepreneurs--and for employees who want to think like entrepreneurs. It will help you unleash the innate creative genius inside you.

Every industry has its sacred cows and accepted practices. These are often based upon foundational premises that are no longer valid--if they ever were.

Visit RandyGage.com

THE TEXTBOOK ON GETTING RICH

RISKY IS THE NEW SAFE

Risky is the New Safe

A thought-provoking manifesto for risk takers. Disruptive technology, accelerating speed of change and economic upheaval are changing the game. The same tired, old conventional thinking won't get you to success today. Risky Is the New Safe will change the way you look at everything!

Visit NetworkMarketingTimes.com

MANIFEST PROSPERITY IN YOUR LIFE

THE PROSPERITY SERIES

The Prosperity Series

You are meant to be healthy, happy and prosperous. Once you recognize and accept this, it is simply a case of learning the principles that abundance is based on. In this insightful series, you will move from lack consciousness to living in the light of true abundance.

Visit RandyGage.com

BUILD A MASSIVE ORGANIZATION

DUPLICATION NATION

Duplication Nation

This is the most advanced training on the science of building an organization that has ever been offered. It is a complete step-by-step system to growing an organization. It can help the industry beginner all the way to the seasoned professional. 12 audio CDs or 12 video DVDs, study guide and bonus business building materials.

Visit NetworkMarketingTimes.com

STOP GETTING REJECTED!

THE LIFESTYLE FREEDOM PACK

The Lifestyle Freedom Pack

Use the Lifestyle Freedom Pack to screen out non-prospects and qualify the real ones. This is an opportunity meeting in an album!

Visit NetworkMarketingTimes.com

MASSIVE DUPLICATION STRATEGIES
HOW TO BECOME A MLM ROCKSTAR

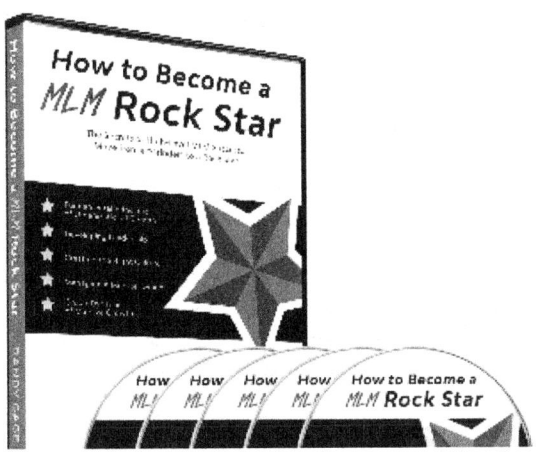

How to Become a MLM Rock Star

5 CD album. This is the true "Insider" info that Randy used to build one of the fastest growing organizations ever seen in the industry. This is NOT a training album on how to get a prospect's phone number, or product retailing tips! This is the high level, leadership and culture stuff, the information you need to lead a massive organization and guide it through exponential growth.

Visit NetworkMarketingTimes.com

SECRETS OF NETWORK MARKETING

VOLUME 1

Secrets Network Marketing Success Vol. 1

This powerful album from Randy Gage will help you discover how to create powerful duplication in your Network Marketing organization. It's the latest information on what's working today in the new economy. This is a 'must have" resource for anyone that is serious about MLM success.

Visit NetworkMarketingTimes.com

SECRETS OF NETWORK MARKETING
VOLUME 2

Secrets Network Marketing Success Vol. 2

This dynamic new resource is just what you need to explode your network marketing business! In Volume One you learned how to grow a strong team. Now in this follow up resource you'll discover how to get duplication into play so your bonus check can multiply! You'll learn exactly how Randy Gage built an organization that made him a living legend, and one of the top income earners of our time.

Visit NetworkMarketingTimes.com

CPSIA information can be obtained
at www.ICGtesting.com
Printed in the USA
FSOW04n1757260917
39219FS